THE GIFTS
OF TONGUES
AND OF
PROPHECY

THE GIFTS
OF TONGUES
AND OF
PROPHECY

Forasmuch as ye are zealous
of spiritual *gifts*,
seek that ye may excel
to the edifying of the church

I Corinthians 14:12

JOHN METCALFE

THE JOHN METCALFE PUBLISHING TRUST
Church road, Tylers Green, Penn, Buckinghamshire

Printed and Published by
The John Metcalfe Publishing Trust
Church Road, Tylers Green
Penn, Buckinghamshire

–

Distributed by Trust Representatives
and Agents world-wide

–

–

First Published 2001
Reprinted 2011

–

ISBN 978 1 870039 86 4

–

CONTENTS

THE GIFTS OF TONGUES AND OF PROPHECY

The Manifestation of the Gifts, I Corinthians 14:1-40

SINCE this is a corrective passage, the apostle handles the matter under four distinct heads:

FIRST: PAUL COMPARES THE USEFULNESS OF PROPHECY WITH THE LIMITATION OF TONGUES, I CORINTHIANS 14:1-25.

SECOND: HE DIRECTS THE ORDERLY MANIFESTATION OF GIFTS WHEN COMING TOGETHER IN THE ECCLESIA, I CORINTHIANS 14:26-33.

THIRD: THE APOSTLE FORBIDS WOMEN TO SPEAK OR ASK QUESTIONS, BUT TO BE UNDER OBEDIENCE IN THE ECCLESIA, I CORINTHIANS 14:34,35.

FOURTH: PAUL STRESSES THAT THE WORD OF GOD CAME *UNTO* THEM, NOT AROSE *FROM* THEM. THEN, LET EVERY ONE OF THEM ACKNOWLEDGE WITHOUT GAINSAYING THAT THE DOCTRINE AND DISCIPLINE OF I CORINTHIANS 14:1-40 *ARE THE COMMANDMENTS OF THE LORD*, VV. 36-40.

To proceed:

FIRST: PAUL COMPARES THE USEFULNESS OF PROPHECY WITH THE LIMITATION OF TONGUES, I CORINTHIANS 14:1-25.

'Follow after love, and desire spiritual gifts, but rather that ye may prophesy', verse 1. The word 'gifts'—in italics in the Authorized Version—is an interpolation.

The Greek is very difficult to render precisely in English: spirituality; what pertains to the spirit; spirituals. Perhaps. But like 'what is spiritual', all these are clumsy in translation.

If I were to give the literal impression, I should read: 'Pursue love, and be zealous of spirituality, but rather that ye may prophesy.' But by 'spirituality' in this place Paul refers to their giving themselves over to spiritual impressions, resulting in unintelligible sounds.

Hence he says immediately: 'For he that speaketh with a tongue, speaketh not unto men, but unto God: for no man understandeth him; howbeit in the spirit he speaketh mysteries.'

Mysteries indeed, not only to others but apparently to himself also, since 'my'—own; let alone others—'understanding is unfruitful', verse 14.

Nevertheless, carried away in emotional response to spiritual impulse, the tongue is loosed beyond control of either understanding or judgment, either to him who speaks, or to those that hear.

2

The Gifts of Tongues and of Prophecy

In no case does Paul suggest foreign languages in Chapter 14: it is clear that what is heard is out of control—quite deliberately, however spiritual the cause—and unintelligible to *anyone* save an hypothetical interpreter.

The most charitable view one can take of verse 2 is that the one speaking in tongues is overwhelmed beyond control by divine and spiritual mysteries.

Paul is saying, If so, evidently it is still possible to control the tongue, whilst retaining the divine impression, and by so doing edify the whole *ecclesia*: that is, '*rather* that ye may prophesy.' Because he that prophesieth speaketh unto men—so that thus they can understand and follow what has been received—'to edification, and exhortation, and comfort.'

Whereas, verse 4, for all the noise made to no purpose for the hearers, he that speaks in a tongue edifies no one but himself. But he that controls his spirit, and declares the mystery intelligibly—which Paul calls 'prophesying'—edifieth *the whole ecclesia*.

Which is preferable? The apostle makes abundantly clear which is preferable, verse 4.

As to being wholly given to what is spiritual, so as to be zealous of receiving what is from the Spirit, such was the value that the apostle clearly placed on their earnest zeal that he desires no check to be put upon *this*, even though it meant for the time present that they all *should* continue speaking with tongues: without any loss to their enthusiasm he seeks to turn the same zeal in them towards prophecy. For surely he detested the least appearance of that dead and inert apathy which the Lord describes as 'lukewarmness'.

Yet for all that, whilst encouraging their fervour, still, *for their own mutual profit*, he would direct that same zealous spirituality into the intelligible utterance of what each one received from the Spirit.

3

'I would that ye all spake with tongues, but rather that ye prophesied: for greater is he that prophesieth than he that speaketh with tongues, except he interpret, that the *ecclesia* may receive edifying', verse 5. But if he interpret, Why the tongue first? for, to all intents and purposes, the interpretation then becomes prophecy!

Suppose *Paul* did what *they* were doing. If he came to them, would they wish *his* speech to be gibberish like theirs, of which they could understand not a word? They would not. No, because that would lose all the value of the life-giving apostolic ministry of the new testament by which they had been begotten of God.

Then—though on a lesser plane—Why do among themselves, what they could not bear from him, if he came to them? 'Now, brethren, if *I* come unto you speaking with tongues, what shall *I* profit you?', verse 6. Profit them? In such a case, no more than the same thing was of profit among themselves. Can they not see this obvious lesson?

But if Paul came speaking to them either by revelation, or by knowledge, or by prophesying, or by doctrine, clearly and intelligibly, so that all understood, how profitable *this* would prove to be.

Will they then cast aside such inestimable blessing for meaningless and incoherent babbling? No they will not. Then why do to themselves in Paul's absence what they would not wish him to do to them were he present?

Using the illustration of a pipe—or flute—then of an harp, and finally a trumpet, Paul signifies the absolute necessity of intelligible sounds in order to communicate to others.

Such instruments are useless of themselves, being without life. That is, unless one either blow air, pluck with the fingers, or sound through the mouthpiece.

However, this alone produces nothing save a tedious monotone, a jangling discord, or a raucous blast: meaningless sounds from living men through dead instruments.

But once the flautist, blowing through the pipe, uses his expertise appropriately to stop the holes with his fingers, then what ordered tones in sequence delight the ear.

Or else the harpist plucking the strings with cunning, selecting and moderating each in turn, or running a part or the whole in a kind of liquid flow: then how lovely the harmony to the hearers.

But in each of these cases the arrangement of the music must be known beforehand, so that the piper pipes the appointed score with skill, the flautist plays the predetermined notes with accomplished control, and the harpist harps upon his stringed instrument to give a distinctive cadence.

Thus in each case the notes harmonize, and the rhythm blends so as to give forth a sweet melody, a thing impossible save by the foreknowledge of the composition, and hence the control of the sound.

As to the trumpet, everyone knows that the force of air must be directed by the different positioning of the lips in order that clear and distinct notes—both in tone and length—may be trumpeted: 'For if the trumpet give an uncertain sound, who shall prepare himself to the battle?', I Corinthians 14:8.

Now all these things are true of lifeless instruments, namely, that musicians must not just blow aimlessly, or strike chords at random, but must know the score beforehand, taking up the instrument to play skilfully, giving a distinction in the notes played.

If so, how much more should the necessity of regulation in sound apply to those voices which give forth a cacophonous babel of unintelligible discord? Clearly, as with music, all should be *regulated* in order to render an *intelligible* sound, so that every one of the hearers might understand and be edified.

Otherwise, despite that men take up the instrument of the tongue, and for all that they speak through their mouth with the voice, the sound is meaningless to anyone unless it be regulated according to intelligible utterance: 'How shall it be known what is spoken? for ye shall speak into the air', I Corinthians 14:9.

Indeed, since the noises have no signification and the resultant sounds are meaningless gibberish to everyone—including the speaker—the hearers may well say of such a tongue, since they themselves give forth the like incoherent babble—and all at one and the same time—'I shall be unto him that speaketh a barbarian, and he that speaketh shall be a barbarian unto me', I Corinthians 14:7-11.

'Even so ye' continues the apostle; that is, 'even' as with the figure of the tuneless and discordant pipe, harp, or trumpet, 'so ye' bawling at each other like barbarians, oblivious of one another's language, raising your voices one at the other—as if you can make up for incomprehension by increasing the volume to a crescendo—thus create a situation little short of ludicrous: nevertheless, 'Even so ye'.

'Even so ye, forasmuch as ye are zealous of spiritualities, seek that ye may excel to the edifying of the *ecclesia*', just as musicians who know their parts and play their instruments accordingly, and as those who speak the same language.

If so, on the one hand as opposed to a discordant cacophony, and on the other, as distinct from two alien barbarians who rant at each other meaninglessly, none knowing the tongue of the other.

'Wherefore let him that speaketh in a tongue pray that he may interpret', verse 13. But in such a case what of the following verse: 'If I pray in a tongue, my spirit prayeth, *but my under-standing is unfruitful*'? But if my understanding is unfruitful, How can I possibly interpret? Yet if I *could* interpret, and my understanding *were* fruitful, then *that* would eliminate the use of the tongue in the *first* place.

And if, after all, I *were* able to interpret *afterwards*, then – given the hypothesis – such an interpretation would be tanta-mount to prophecy. And, saith Paul – as opposed to tongues – prophecy would be for the edification of all. In that case, Why the tongues?

Clearly, though addressed never so gently, the implication of the apostle is inescapable.

And likewise, What of this: 'If any man speak in a tongue ... let one' – that is, *another* one – 'interpret'? see verse 27. By all that has been said already, even to the most prejudiced, three things intrude themselves.

First, if the understanding of the one who speaks in a tongue be unfruitful, it follows of necessity that this means that *he* knows not *what* he says. It is highly doubtful – his understanding being unfruitful – that he even knows what he *means*. Then, How can he possibly interpret to others? verses 13,14.

Second, if a man may only speak in a tongue – in the *ecclesia* – provided *another* interprets – the idea of his own unfruitful understanding enabling him to be his own interpreter being merely hypothetical – then he is *not* to interpret what he him-self spoke in a tongue. See verse 13 *cf* verses 27,28.

Third, even in the case of a man wishing to speak in a tongue in the *ecclesia*, since he may only do so under the condition that another interprets thereafter, *de facto* he is prevented in his wish *because of the impossibility of his knowing in advance whether the interpretation will be given to another or not.*

So that whilst carefully nurturing the spiritual zeal of the Corinthians, and doing nothing to dampen their ardour, nevertheless the apostle, both by his advocacy for the superiority of prophecy, and by the discipline he administers on the exercise of tongues in the *ecclesia*, whilst under no sense forbidding it as such – indeed laying down ordinances which, given an interpreter, allows for it – yet still, their obedience to these ordinances being granted, it is difficult to see how the use of tongues in the *ecclesia* would be possible thereafter.

Hence in the next verses Paul unites the spiritual enthusiasm– one might almost say abandon – in which the Corinthians' emotions, if not passions, were carried away by the intensity of their feelings, with the sobriety and solid control of their *nous*– for so the Greek reads – a word better translated 'mentality' than 'understanding':

'For if I pray in a tongue, my spirit prayeth' – through the excitement of the emotions and passions from spiritual impressions – 'but my *nous*' – my mentality – 'is unfruitful', verse 14.

Why, Paul? Because it is *all* spiritual excitement without *any* comprehending mentality.

That is, I do not know *what* I am saying. I know only what I am feeling. Then, bring both feeling and mentality together under control: 'What is it then? I will pray with the spirit, and I will pray with the *nous*' – mentality – 'also: I will sing with the spirit, and I will sing with the *nous* also.'

But if not, What? 'Else when thou shalt bless with the spirit'– carried away in song or blessing beyond comprehensible words – 'how shall he that occupieth the place of the uninstructed'– uninstructed, that is, in just *what* is going on in such meetings – 'say Amen at thy giving of thanks, seeing he knoweth not'– Greek, *has no idea of* – 'what thou sayest?'

How could he know? It is all unintelligible babel to him.

'For verily'–Paul does not doubt it–'*thou* givest thanks well, but *the other* is not edified.' Yet the edification of others–in the *ecclesia*–is the object of *all* vocal activity, I Corinthians 14:14-17.

For their encouragement, both in private and the assembly–lest they feel rebuked, or disconsolate, over this apostolic–but most considerate–discipline in the Spirit, Paul adds, 'I thank my God, I speak with tongues more than ye all', verse 18.

But what did the apostle actually *mean* by this? The same kind of tongues as they meant? Perhaps; yet certainly not in the *ecclesia*.

Because immediately he states, 'tongues are for *a sign*'–which was hardly the case with the Corinthians–besides, 'a sign, *not to them that believe*', verse 22. Wherefore it is hardly likely that Paul gave forth in tongues *as they did*.

To be consistent with verse 22, verse 18 must suppose that Paul spake in tongues more than they all *to them that believe not*.

Then, in what tongues? For example, the Hebrew tongue, incomprehensible to most of the Corinthians, but not to those unbelievers at Jerusalem: 'And when there was made a great silence, he'–Paul–'spake unto them in *the Hebrew tongue*'.

Besides this, he spoke Greek–preaching the evangel to unbelievers in that tongue–and used the same language to write his epistles; besides this, there is a strong probability from the range of his journeys that he spoke in the varied Greek dialects.

Again, being a citizen of Cilicia, dwelling in the city of Tarsus, there can be no doubt but that he had the tongue of that people also by it preaching to them that believed not.

Once more there can be little question but that Paul spoke Latin, not only from his being a free-born Roman, but also from his years spent in the city of Rome. Hence his ability to converse freely with Romans, whether the centurion and chief captain at Jerusalem, the Romans at Caesarea, or to Julius, a centurion of Augustus' band, to whom Paul was committed on his journey in custody to Rome.

Indeed, the Romans themselves testified at Jerusalem, 'this man is a Roman', Acts 22:26, and a free-born Roman at that, verse 28. Then can anyone doubt that he would have had the Latin tongue?

And – quite apart from other tongues peculiar to the different peoples to whom he was sent – such as the Syrians of Damascus – is not this 'speaking in tongues more than ye all'? And was not this 'a sign to them that believe not', carrying the evangel intelligibly to them?

Or, if it be a matter of revelations and of spirituality, Paul excelled all, being caught up to the third heaven, hearing unspeakable words, which it was not lawful for a man to utter, II Corinthians 12:2-4.

But if not lawful, Paul would not utter them, no not in any tongue. And if unspeakable, Paul *could* not utter them, since no tongue sufficed to utter what could not be spoken. And what can be more spiritual than that?

Not as if Paul mentioned the incident till writing the second epistle to the Corinthians, from which it is evident that he restrained himself in all things that he might benefit the brethren: 'Yet in the *ecclesia* I had rather speak five words with my *nous*, that by my voice I might teach others also, than ten thousand words in an unknown tongue.'

Whereupon he exhorts the brethren not to be children – or childish – in *intelligence*, but to grasp the reason for what he was saying as *intelligent* men – that is, in mature manhood. See I Corinthians 14:18-20.

At this point therefore he appeals to the scriptures of the prophets: 'In the law it is written, With men of other tongues and other lips will I speak unto this people; and yet for all that will they not hear me, saith the Lord.

'Wherefore tongues are for a sign, not to them that believe, but to them that believe not: but prophesying serveth not for them that believe not, but for them which believe', verses 21,22.

Concerning tongues as a sign to them that believe not, there was nothing incoherent about it: 'And they were all filled with the Holy Ghost, and began to speak *with other tongues*, as the Spirit gave them utterance'–that is *other* than their *own* tongue, or language–'And there were dwelling at Jerusalem Jews, devout men, out of every nation under heaven.

'Now when this was noised abroad, the multitude came together, and were confounded, because that every man heard *them* speak *in his own language.*'

And they, though devout Jews, yet unbelievers, 'marvelled, saying one to another, Behold, are not all these which speak Galileans? and how hear we every man in our own tongue, wherein we were born?

'Parthians, and Medes, and Elamites, and the dwellers in Mesopotamia, and in Judea, and Cappadocia, in Pontus, and Asia, Phrygia, and Pamphylia, in Egypt, and in the parts of Libya about Cyrene, and strangers of Rome, Jews and proselytes, Cretes, and Arabians, we do hear *them* speak *in our tongues* the wonderful works of God', Acts 2:4-11.

Now, *this* was tongues with a witness. And this was tongues with a witness to *unbelievers*. Where *the saints* knew not the tongue in which they spoke, but the interpretation, respectively, was given by the hearing of fifteen different nations, in the tongues wherein they were born.

11

Other cases of tongues, as with Cornelius' company, and those at Ephesus, were likewise a sign, not least to the apostles themselves, that God would justify the Gentiles also – a thing at first unbelievable to them.

Of this Peter, called to account at Jerusalem, could not but testify, saying, 'Forasmuch then as God gave them' – who, from being Gentile unbelievers, were brought to faith – '*the like gift as he did unto us*, who believed on the Lord Jesus Christ; what was I, that I could withstand God?

'When they heard these things' – that what happened to *them*, at Pentecost, had happened *to the Gentiles also* – 'they held their peace.'

Wherefore tongues are for a sign, not to them that believe, but to them that believe not. In which sign, note, the speakers had no knowledge of the tongue which they uttered, and the interpretation came from the unbelieving foreigners who heard.

As to Corinth, this was another thing altogether: it was to *them that believe*, which is all wrong, and turns the scripture upside-down. Besides this, *there was no question of foreign languages.*

It was not a matter of 'Are not all these which speak Corinthians?' It was more a matter of 'Are not all these which babble Barbarians?'

Interpret? They were all too preoccupied with 'speaking in tongues' every man for himself, till there was not one who was left to interpret.

And not to interpret by translating some foreign language *outside*, but to puzzle over 'mysteries' indeed within. Within? But yet, out of all the *ecclesiais* in the new testament, within that peculiar to Corinth alone.

Still, how patient and longsuffering the apostle appears in his ministry, anxious to encourage their zeal, whilst guiding them into a more excellent way, to more edifying prophecy, withal for the time being forbidding nothing at all.

Nevertheless, the truth which he states, without applying it, save leaving it to their *nous*, stands from the day of Pentecost till the end of time: 'Wherefore tongues are for a sign, not to them that believe, but to them that *believe not.*' That is to those without.

As to those *within*, that is, '*them which believe*', in the same verse the apostle sets everything in stark contrast: 'but'–mark that: *but*–'prophesying serveth *not for them that believe not*, but for *them which believe*', I Corinthians 14:21,22.

But for all the great weight of that which the apostle had pleaded up to this point, he makes yet one further appeal to the Corinthians, that they themselves might see good reason for favouring utterance by prophecy, in their own minds being persuaded of the unsuitability of tongues in the meetings of the *ecclesia*.

'If therefore the whole *ecclesia* be come together into one place, and all speak with tongues, and there come in those that are unlearned, or unbelievers, *will they not say that ye are mad?*'

That was their present witness. Mad.

'But if all prophesy, and there come in one that believeth not, or one unlearned, he is convinced of all, he is judged of all: and thus are the secrets of his heart made manifest; and so falling down on his face will worship God, *and report that God is in you of a truth.*'

That was the witness Paul desired for them in the future.

13

Well, What would they? Madness, and the common reputation for it? Or God's indwelling, and the general report that they had become his habitation?

The apostle presents a choice amounting to this: Will they have tongues and madness? or will they have prophecy and sanity? See I Corinthians 14:23-25.

This leads the apostle to the next head in the passage from I Corinthians 14:1-40:

SECOND: HE DIRECTS THE ORDERLY MANIFESTATION OF GIFTS WHEN COMING TOGETHER IN THE *ECCLESIA*, I CORINTHIANS 14:26-33.

From the preceding passages and especially the context it is abundantly evident that 'tongues' were coveted above all by the Corinthians, who had been beguiled into supposing that the use of this gift was the height of spirituality in the *ecclesia*. But it was not.

Nor was this sign – or gift – for them that believe at all, but for them that believe not, Chapter 14:22.

Prophecy, however, was another matter altogether, verses 23-25. Paul had made this crystal clear.

However, he does not forbid tongues: he puts the gift – or sign – in perspective, relegating it to its comparative status and due order according to the ways of God in those apostolic times at the beginning in which he writes.

I say 'apostolic times' for it must be borne in mind constantly that such a period was as unique to the inauguration of the new testament as was the receiving of the law and the signs following the deliverance of Israel from Egypt until the crossing of Jordan into the promised land under the old testament.

14

The *origination* of both testaments, ordained under each respective Apostle, was marked by a period of miracles, signs, and wonders never intended to be repeated in subsequent generations, nor – as the history of Israel demonstrates – *were* they repeated, though they *were* constantly to be had in remembrance.

The cessation of the falling of the manna from heaven; of the water from the Rock which followed them; or of the pillar of cloud and of fire which guided them, did not make the subsequent generations *less* of Israel after they crossed the river of Jordan.

What it did was to make the *continuation of Israel in the doctrine delivered by Moses* to be marked out as divinely given by the unique and distinguishing features manifest at their beginnings. Just so in the new testament.

Now, however, the apostle continues, 'How is it then, brethren? when ye come together, every one of you hath a psalm, hath a doctrine, hath a tongue, hath a revelation, hath an interpretation. Let all things be done unto edifying', Chapter 14:26.

It is essential to grasp the background of this passage, over against the accretions of the ages, layer upon layer, and the accumulation of both traditions and prejudices, under which it has been continually and increasingly buried during the intervening centuries, not least by those who suppose themselves to be so scriptural that they judge everyone *other* than themselves to be guilty of this grotesque form of tumidity.

'How is it then, brethren? when ye come together', verse 26, answers to 'If therefore the whole *ecclesia* be come together into one place', verse 23.

First enquire, If all the brethren, that is, the whole *ecclesia*, be come together in one place, then how on earth can that *place* be called the *ecclesia* or 'church'? It cannot.

The *ecclesia* or 'church' is said to come together *into that place*, not that *the place* into which the *ecclesia* or 'church' came was called by the name of those who came into it! Then, in those apostolic times, all the brethren, the entire *ecclesia*, came together into one place.

But now it is different.

A motley congregation, the majority of which – even by their own standards – are not converted, and the conversion even of the core minority would certainly be questionable by apostolic standards, I say, if these come together on a sectarian basis – that is, on the basis of a 'membership' divided from the unity of one body – into a building more or less conformed to a certain architectural pattern, which they have the temerity to call 'the church' or 'their church', and, at that, with a denominational name appended, What follows?

It *must* follow that *they cannot be* the *ecclesia* or 'church', they themselves bearing a twofold witness against themselves. First, by the misapplication of the term. Second, by the added qualification of their denominational title.

Thus, those of that denomination 'go' to 'their' church. How can this be? Because *the place* into which they come is named deceitfully. Not to say, denominationally.

And, for all their pretensions, I do not see that the substitution of 'meeting' or 'hall' for 'church' *makes the slightest difference unless those who come together do so in the unity of the one body, that is, in the one fellowship which is in the Father, and in his Son Jesus Christ, abiding in the communion of the Holy Ghost.*

For *that* was what Paul meant when he said, 'How is it then, brethren? when ye come together', and, 'If therefore the whole *ecclesia* be come together into one place'.

But what *men* mean by 'going to church' is as far removed from the context of the apostle–and the remotest possibility of any application of his words–as the north pole is distant from the south.

Self-styled 'biblical' congregations may hide this truth–for example by housing-estate style 'modern' halls, or whatever.

But everybody knows what these adapted buildings represent–with their modest hints of some updated 'ecclesiastical' feature or another–just as much as if these were the modern spawn of ancient cathedrals, with which, in practice, the superstition of multitudes associates as being worthy of a like – if lesser – veneration.

And why not? For, within, if not a font, there is a baptistery. If not a sacristy, there is a vestry. If not an altar, there is a table. If not a reading desk, there is a pulpit. If not a priest, there is a pastor. If not a pastor, there are 'speakers'.

And in the minds of worldly, unconverted people–not dispossessed of common sense by the prejudice of religious bias– what is the difference? A difference in kind, but not a difference in substance.

How unlike the times when 'brethren, *ye* come together'! 'How is it then, brethren? when *ye* come together'? For a start, no one brought, or could bring, a bible. The old testament rolls were far and away too inaccessible, and the hand written and copied books of the new testament–such as they were at that time and place–were as yet neither collated nor assembled.

At most–and that but rarely–there would be an apostolic epistle written to them or to others nearby to be read by an able brother to the entire assembly. But no one individual possessed his own copy, much less his own bible, and certainly not his own new testament.

Neither had they any written psalms, songs, or hymns. In fact, they came empty handed, having no books of *any* kind to bring, or to find laid out for them on arrival.

Whatever was written was written by the Holy Ghost on fleshy tables of the heart.

As to writings on tables of stone, or rolls of parchment, apart from unavailability, the balance of probabilities weighs heavily against the majority of the Corinthians–not to say, the saints of the new testament, many of whom were slaves–being able to read or write at all.

Then, all depended upon the anointing by which they needed not that any man teach them, namely, the inward spiritual writing on the heart by the Holy Ghost from heaven, *and the inspired memory of what they had received from the preaching and teaching of the apostolic ministers of the new testament.*

Hence, in coming together in one place, the apostle's insistence upon the participation, verification, and witness of at least *two*, or, appropriately, *three*, when ministering any gift among themselves. This was nothing less than imperative.

It is an absolutely vital fact to be fixed in the mind that they depended upon the Holy Ghost to bring to their remembrance what had been taught to them, just as much as the accurate memory of those psalms, hymns, and spiritual songs agreeable to the doctrine of Christ.

Hence the necessity of verification by another in the exercise of any one gift: 'If any man speak in an unknown tongue, *let it be by two, or at the most three*'–far from the entire number!– '*and that by course*'–not all at once!–'and let *another* interpret', I Corinthians 14:27.

Again, 'Let the prophets speak *two or three*, and *let the other judge*. If any thing be revealed to another that sitteth by, *let the first hold his peace*', verses 29,30.

Thus, since *memory* was the crucial issue, the apostle enjoins an order in which *corroboration was assured* by at least one, if not two, others.

Observe likewise his patience and gentleness with the Corinthians in the allowance of tongues *within* the assembly, and *to* believers, despite what he had declared in verse 22, not to say verses 23-25.

However, since his allowance of tongues was conditional upon an interpreter, it is difficult to see how tongues could be exercised in the assembly, since it would have been impossible for one so speaking to know beforehand whether an interpretation would follow or not.

In any event *the principle* of two or at the most three in the exercise of any one gift held good, and *that* was the main issue.

Nor does *our* possession of a complete bible – old and new testament – together with the – now at last available – invaluable psalms, hymns, and spiritual songs, *alter the principle of dependence upon the interior witness and inwriting of the Holy Ghost leading us also, where reference to what is written takes the place of remembrance of what had been spoken.*

The same injunctions still apply, because they are principles in their nature, and, if so, enduring in their application.

Once again notice the wording: 'How is it then, brethren? when ye come together, every one of you hath a psalm, hath a doctrine, hath a tongue, hath a revelation, hath an interpretation', verse 26.

And again, 'If therefore the whole *ecclesia* be come together into one place', verse 23. Note carefully that this was *the* meeting of the saints, of all the brethren, of the whole *ecclesia*.

No suggestion exists that the taking of the Lord's supper in fellowship after their meal together was at a *different* time or place. The inference is that it was at *this* time and place.

But *the functioning of the gifts in conveying the word of God by the Holy Ghost through the appropriate members of the body transcended all.* Whatever else may have taken place when 'the whole *ecclesia* be come together into one place', or when brethren 'come together', the declaration of the word of the truth of the evangel was paramount.

The Supper – or 'Breaking of Bread on Lord's Day Morning' as some so unscripturally, unsoundly, and inaccurately denominate it – or the so-called 'Gospel Meeting'; the Prayer Meeting; or the Meeting for Fellowship, and suchlike: all these things might and perhaps in some cases did accompany that paramountcy: *but nothing equalled it.*

Whatever *was* ordained, accompanied it. *This* was *the* meeting of the saints; of all the brethren; of the whole *ecclesia*, and, it appears this involved *everything*.

Indeed, the *conception* of this passage leads to the supposition of *one* meeting – *this* meeting – for everything, and, in all likelihood, *every night of the week*, cessation from work permitting. Mark that well, in this apostate day of apathy and lukewarm half-heartedness.

In contrast, then, in those early times everything that they did was all done *in one and the same meeting*, and at that 'daily', when 'the whole *ecclesia* be come together into one place', and, 'brethren, when ye come together.'

I repeat: *then* not only was all in one, but in all probability it was *every day*. Why repeat this? Because it *should* be repeated, and that in our own times.

Carefully notice the nature of the coming together of the *ecclesia* in the exercise and manifestation of the gifts of the Spirit in the body of Christ. What appears so clearly is that it *was* the *body of Christ* that came together 'into one place' and as 'brethren'. Hence there followed the *manifestation of the gifts of the Spirit in the body, as assembled in one for edification.*

What followed? 'Every one of you hath a psalm, hath a doctrine, hath a tongue, hath a revelation, hath an interpretation.' And, since it *was* 'every one of you' the apostle admonishes the brethren to wait in due order, that all might be edified: 'Let all things be done unto edifying', verse 26.

Here there is not the slightest resemblance to divided memberships coming together each in its own separate quarter to hear a hired priest, 'ordained' minister, 'trained' pastor, or presumptuous 'brother'. No priest, minister, pastor, or usurper appears in any place whatsoever in this passage dealing exhaustively and apostolically with the coming together of the body of Christ into one.

No such grotesque impositions as have mushroomed since, existed in the one *ecclesia* of God. The gifts of the Spirit in and from the members of the body in and of themselves provided the whole of the ministry and the entirety of the edification. This is not to say that the apostles were then present, or that their giving the apostolic ministry is the subject of this passage.

It is to say that *this* is the apostles' doctrine for the gathering together into one place of the *ecclesia*, where *this* answers to the manifestation of the gifts of the Spirit on the part of those to whom such gifts were given, for the edification of the whole.

That is, 'Every one hath' by the same Spirit, that which harmonized with all other manifest gifts for the edification of the entire body, and in the agreement and unity of the conscience and judgment of every one of the brethren.

'Every one hath.' Not 'the pastor hath'; not 'the priest hath'; not 'the minister hath'; not 'every presumptuous usurper hath': quite apart from *such fictional impositions and impostors as these, plying their trade in the divisions outside of the body, nevertheless within the body,* 'every one hath'.

As to 'the pastor': there was no pastor. As to the 'priests': they had passed away with the old covenant. As to Brethren imitations: there were no Brethren imitations.

As to the booked and arranged Speakers, such things were unheard of in that 'whole church come together into one place', when 'brethren, ye come together' and 'every one'—gifted by the Holy Ghost in one body—'hath a psalm, hath a doctrine, hath a tongue, hath a revelation, hath an interpretation', I Corinthians 14:26.

Nothing else existed in the *ecclesia*, the body of Christ. No, nor in this entire epistle, namely, that epistle singled out and devoted to expounding once and for all the manifestation of the gifts of the indwelling Spirit in the coming together of the *ecclesia*, the body of Christ, into one place.

Then, when the brethren were thus come together, one rule prevailed: 'Let all things be done unto edifying.' That is, not all at once, but one after the other. And not one gift alone but each differing *charisma* in due order unto edification.

Now for the time being allowing for tongues in the assembling of the *ecclesia*, despite that the drift of the context had been to the contrary, the exceeding gentleness of the apostle, his moderation towards their excess falling short of outright prohibition or sudden closure; the apostle continues.

'If any man speak in an unknown tongue, let it be by two, or at the most three, and that by course'—as opposed to everyone presuming the same gift, and that all at once—'and let one interpret.'

But, as has been said, How shall the two, or at most three, speaking in tongues by course, *know* that they will be followed by that interpretation without which they are to keep silence? 'But if there be no interpreter, let him keep silence in the *ecclesia*; and let him speak to himself, and to God', verse 28.

Next, Paul comes to prophecy. The same principle applies, though the gift differs: 'Let the prophets speak two or three, and let the other judge. If any thing be revealed to another that sitteth by'–who has judged by the Spirit what had been prophesied–'let the first hold his peace.'

For such a revelation, enlarging or contracting the previous prophecy, would be all one as if he that received the revelation were a prophet also: 'For ye may all prophesy one by one'–one *after* the other–'that all may learn, and all may be comforted.

'And the spirits of the prophets are subject to the prophets.' If so, then each must receive from and submit to the furtherance and enlargement of others in sequence, not claiming that the spirit in him gave him the right to interrupt whomsoever followed.

On the contrary, the spirit of the prophets being subject to the prophets, the previous speaker must meekly receive the further revelation of the other prophets, added to his own contribution, each in his own order, so that the judgment of all being edified and comforted by this witness of diversities of gifts–but the same Spirit–the entire *ecclesia* is comforted.

See I Corinthians 12:4 and likewise I Corinthians 14:29-33. 'For God is not the author of confusion, but of peace, as in all the *ecclesiais* of the saints.'

Such a verse, embracing that commensurate discipline following from the apostolic authority through which the Lord himself directed the doctrine and fellowship received by all the *ecclesiais* of the saints, brings Paul to the next revelation of the new testament commanding the coming together of the *ecclesia*, that is, the gathering together into one place of the body of Christ.

THIRD: THE APOSTLE FORBIDS WOMEN TO SPEAK OR ASK QUESTIONS, BUT TO BE UNDER OBEDIENCE IN THE *ECCLESIA*, I CORINTHIANS 14:34,35.

Further to the truth that 'God is not the author of confusion, but of peace, as in all the *ecclesiais* of the saints' the apostle immediately follows with the commandment of the Lord, and word of God, necessary for the achievement and continuance of such a divinely given peace, namely, 'Let your women keep silence in the *ecclesiais*' – not just the *ecclesia* at Corinth, note: it is not in the singular, *ecclesia*; it is plural, '*ecclesiais*'.

Then, this commandment of the Lord necessarily extends *everywhere* and to *all generations* – 'for it is not permitted unto them to speak; but they are commanded to be under obedience, as also saith the law', verse 34.

The law? Where in the law? The *Torah* for instance. *Genesis* for example. Of this, recorded in the first book of Moses, 'nature itself teacheth you', as saith the apostle, I Corinthians 11:2,11-16.

Teacheth you what? The difference between the creation of the man; the forming of the woman from the man; the woman being deceived; the bringing in of the Fall – because she *would* answer the serpent, and *would not* ask her husband – *and the difference between the man and the woman before God, and especially since the judgment of the Fall*, Genesis chapters 2 and 3, concerning which the apostle teaches the truth, I Timothy 2:11-15.

The law also confirms this truth and commandment elsewhere in the *Torah*, not least with the offerings and the feasts – which the *men* of Israel were to offer – and for the same reason. 'Thrice in the year shall all your *menchildren* appear before the Lord GOD, the God of Israel', Exodus 34:23.

It is true that in special circumstances there were offerings for women – as in childbirth or an issue – but although these were given by the woman *they must be offered by the priest*.

Indeed, as to all the chief and continual offerings it is 'If any *man* of you bring an offering', Leviticus 1:2. And, at that, though the man did much, the priest did more, actually bringing the offering both to the altar and before the LORD.

As to women, they did nothing; and as for priestesses, they belonged to the detestable abominations of the heathen, from which Israel was utterly to separate himself, and which he was perpetually to abhor and abominate.

As also saith the law. Not to mention the gospel. Then, 'Let your women *keep silence* in the *ecclesiais*: for it is not permitted unto them to speak; but they are *commanded* to be *under obedience*, as also'–that is, *besides* the evangel; *as well as* the gospel; so *also*– 'saith the law', I Corinthians 14:34.

'And if they'–the women–'will learn any thing, let them ask their husbands at home'–which is what Eve did not do; but Sarah did, who embodied this meek submission and subjection to God, to Christ, and to her husband, as the apostle Peter carefully instructs you, I Peter 3:5,6.

As to the rest, the apostle Paul adds *'for it is a shame for women to speak in the ecclesia'*, I Corinthians 14:35.

FOURTH: PAUL STRESSES THAT THE WORD OF GOD CAME *UNTO* THEM, NOT AROSE *FROM* THEM. THEN, LET EVERY ONE OF THEM ACKNOWLEDGE WITHOUT GAINSAYING THAT THE DOCTRINE AND DISCIPLINE OF I CORINTHIANS 14:1-40 *ARE THE COMMANDMENTS OF THE LORD*, VERSES 36-40.

With a mixture of asperity and indignation the apostle allows some of the outrage that he feels to appear in the closing verses. 'What?' How this bursts out!

And so it would again today against every know-all so-called 'brother' with a head full of dead scriptures–of whatever version–

and a heart full of presumption–over whatever notions–who thinks that such impudence can supersede the four vital questions, 'How then shall they call on him in whom they have not believed? and how shall they believe in him of whom they have not heard?

'And how shall they hear without a preacher?'–mark that: *hear*, not *read*; and a *preacher*, not the *dead letter*: the Ethiopian eunuch had that; Cornelius had that–'And how shall they preach, *except they be sent?*'

And if *sent*, then such divine, heavenly apostolic ministers as these who bring the word of faith which we preach, and who bring it unto us with the Holy Ghost sent down from heaven, ought to be received with all heartfelt humility and submission.

And if these are sent to bring to us the word of faith, How come you deny them, pick up a bible–of whatever version, about which background you know nothing–and without fail confound it, add to it, subtract from it, multiply it, divide it, and yet profess it, *when you were never sent, no, nor ever received any one thing from God out of heaven to bring to the people?*

What? Came the word of God out from you? No, it did not. It came unto you only; or else, properly received and rightly so-called, *it never came unto you at all*. For you can be sure of this: *the dead letter in your hands will never be a substitute for this mighty work of the living God in those who are sent by the Holy Ghost.*

However, that word *was* sent, and it *did* come to the Corinthians, and hence, their conversion was a living testimony to the power of God. And, notwithstanding that later they erred, yet despite all, he who was sent to them in the power of God still had such a divinely given hope of their recovery, for all their need of so much and varied correction, that he was not to be disappointed.

'Or came it'–the word of God–'unto you only?' What can they do, who must own the sending of Paul to Corinth, the

Lord saying to him in a vision in the night, 'Be not afraid, but speak, and hold not thy peace: for I am with thee, and no man shall set on thee to hurt thee: for I have much people in this city', Acts 18:9,10?

They can but bow in shame and contrition of heart. And what can *they* do, who, unconverted, nowadays lift themselves up, every man unsent, who must book speakers, filling up the vacant dates themselves by both necessity and presumption, thrusting themselves into that to which God never called them.

And what? Being unconverted, they gain no converts. Being uncalled, they cannot call others. Being unsent, they can never arrive. Being dead, they can give no life.

But putting on a show, they act out and do all that they can, with as bright a pretence as possible, attracting those as light and chaffy, as vain and carnal as themselves, worldlings all, till the whole is got together in the flesh over a dead bible – of whatever version – and a frothy form of religion.

But it was never so at Corinth. What? Paul declares that the word of God, in life and power, *came unto them only*. It never came out from them. Which is what they could not deny, and did not deny, but humbly confessed, as witnessed by the second epistle to the Corinthians from Paul, an apostle of Jesus Christ by the will of God, and Timothy, brother, unto the *ecclesia* of God which is at Corinth, with all the saints which are in all Achaia.

Here it is evident that even the most disputatious and contentious had been brought to a broken spirit and contrite heart, being subdued of God, and made submissive in the Holy Ghost.

But first Paul says, 'If any man think himself to be a prophet, or spiritual, let him acknowledge that the things' – all the things, every one of the things, in the whole epistle without exception, and especially in chapter 14 – 'that I write unto you *are the commandments of the Lord.*'

But should anyone question anything whatsoever, then 'Ignorance' was writ large across his forehead: and who will hear anything from such a man as that? Since he is obdurate, let him be dismissed. 'If any man be ignorant, let him be ignorant.'

In conclusion the apostle conveys his solicitude concerning them, studying the welfare of his own dear children in the faith, full of helpfulness and encouragement.

'Wherefore, brethren, covet to prophesy, and forbid not to speak with tongues. Let all things be done decently and in order', I Corinthians 14:39,40.

This ends the chapter, and the entire eleventh division of the epistle.

JOHN METCALFE

INDEX

TO OTHER PUBLICATIONS

PSALMS, HYMNS AND SPIRITUAL SONGS

Thoroughly revised Second Edition, Third Printing
superior binding by Green Street Bindery

THE PSALMS

OF THE

OLD TESTAMENT

The Psalms of the Old Testament is an original rendering into verse from the Authorized Version, which presents the psalms in the purest scriptural form possible for singing. Here, for the first time, divine names are rendered as and when they occur in the scripture, the distinction between LORD and Lord has been preserved, and every essential point of doctrine and experience appears with unique perception and fidelity.

Price £4.25 *(postage extra)*
(hard-case binding, head and foot bands,
laminated dust-jacket)
Printed by the John Metcalfe Publishing Trust
ISBN 978 1 870039 75 8

Thoroughly revised second edition
Over five thousand copies sold

SPIRITUAL SONGS

FROM THE

FOUR EVANGELISTS

The *Spiritual Songs from the Four Evangelists*, the result of years of painstaking labour, is an original translation into verse from the Authorized Version, including numerous corrections from the Greek of the Received Text, presenting essential parts from the evangelists in the purest scriptural form for singing. The careful selections from Matthew, Mark, Luke, and John, set forth in metrical verse, enable one to sing 'the word of Christ' as if from the scripture itself, 'richly and in all wisdom', and, above all, in a way that facilitates worship in songs of unprecedented fidelity.

The *Spiritual Songs from the Four Evangelists* is the central part of a trilogy written by John Metcalfe, the first part of which is entitled *The Psalms of the Old Testament*, and the last, *The Hymns of the New Testament*. These titles provide unique and accurate metrical versions of passages from the psalms, the evangelists, and the new testament epistles respectively, and are intended to be used together in the worship of God.

Price £2.50 (*postage extra*)
(hard-case binding, dust-jacket)
Printed, sewn and bound
by the John Metcalfe Publishing Trust
ISBN 978 1 870039 90 1

Thoroughly revised second edition

Over five thousand copies sold

THE HYMNS

OF THE

NEW TESTAMENT

The Hymns of the New Testament, the result of years of painstaking labour, is an original translation into verse from the Authorized Version, including numerous corrections from the Greek of the Received Text, presenting essential parts of the new testament epistles in the purest scriptural form for singing. The careful selection from the book of Acts to that of Revelation, set forth in metrical verse, enables the singer to sing 'the word of Christ' as if from the scripture itself, 'richly and in all wisdom', and, above all, in a way that facilitates worship in song of unprecedented fidelity.

The Hymns of the New Testament is the last part of a trilogy written by John Metcalfe, the first part of which is entitled *The Psalms of the Old Testament*, and the next, *Spiritual Songs from the Four Evangelists*. These titles provide unique and accurate metrical versions of passages from the psalms, the evangelists, and the new testament epistles respectively, and are intended to be used together in the worship of God.

Price £2.50 *(postage extra)*
(hard-case binding, dust-jacket)
Printed, sewn and bound
by the John Metcalfe Publishing Trust
ISBN 978 1 870039 81 9

'THE APOSTOLIC FOUNDATION
OF THE
CHRISTIAN CHURCH' SERIES

Third printing

Over ten thousand copies sold

FOUNDATIONS UNCOVERED

THE APOSTOLIC FOUNDATION
OF THE
CHRISTIAN CHURCH

Volume I

Foundations Uncovered is the introduction to the major series: 'The Apostolic Foundation of the Christian Church'.

Rich in truth, the Introduction deals comprehensively with the foundation of the apostolic faith under the descriptive titles: The Word, The Doctrine, The Truth, The Gospel, The Faith, The New Testament, and The Foundation.

The contents of the book reveal: The Fact of the Foundation; The Foundation Uncovered; What the Foundation is not; How the Foundation is Described; and, Being Built upon the Foundation.

'This book comes with the freshness of a new Reformation.'

Price 75p *(postage extra)*
Paperback 110 pages (Laminated cover)
Printed, sewn and bound
by the John Metcalfe Publishing Trust
ISBN 978 0 9506366 5 8

Thoroughly revised and extensively rewritten
Second edition, Third printing
Over ten thousand copies sold

THE BIRTH OF JESUS CHRIST

THE APOSTOLIC FOUNDATION
OF THE
CHRISTIAN CHURCH

Volume II

'The very spirit of adoration and worship rings through the pages of *The Birth of Jesus Christ*.

'The author expresses with great clarity the truths revealed to him in his study of holy scriptures at depth. We are presented here with a totally lofty view of the Incarnation.

'John Metcalfe is to be classed amongst the foremost expositors of our age; and his writings have about them that quality of timelessness that makes me sure they will one day take their place among the heritage of truly great Christian works.'

From a review by Rev. David Catterson.

'Uncompromisingly faithful to scripture ... has much to offer which is worth serious consideration ... deeply moving.'

The Expository Times.

Price 95p *(postage extra)*
Paperback 160 pages (Laminated cover)
Printed, sewn and bound
by the John Metcalfe Publishing Trust
ISBN 978 1 870039 48 2

Thoroughly revised and extensively rewritten
Second edition (hardback), Third printing
Over ten thousand copies sold

THE MESSIAH

THE APOSTOLIC FOUNDATION
OF THE
CHRISTIAN CHURCH

Volume III

The Messiah is a spiritually penetrating and entirely original exposition of Matthew chapter one to chapter seven from the trenchant pen of John Metcalfe.

Matthew Chapters One to Seven

GENEALOGY · BIRTH · STAR OF BETHLEHEM
HEROD · FLIGHT TO EGYPT · NAZARETH
JOHN THE BAPTIST · THE BAPTIST'S MINISTRY
JESUS' BAPTISM · ALL RIGHTEOUSNESS FULFILLED
HEAVEN OPENED · THE SPIRIT'S DESCENT
THE TEMPTATION OF JESUS IN THE WILDERNESS
JESUS' MANIFESTATION · THE CALLING · THE TRUE DISCIPLES
THE BEATITUDES · THE SERMON ON THE MOUNT

'Something of the fire of the ancient Hebrew prophet ...... Metcalfe has spiritual and expository potentials of a high order.'
The Life of Faith.

Price £7.75 *(postage extra)*
Hardback 420 pages
Laminated bookjacket
Printed, sewn and bound
by the John Metcalfe Publishing Trust
ISBN 978 1 870039 51 2

Second edition (hardback)
Over five thousand copies sold

THE SON OF GOD AND SEED OF DAVID

THE APOSTOLIC FOUNDATION
OF THE
CHRISTIAN CHURCH

Volume IV

The Son of God and Seed of David is the fourth volume in the major work entitled 'The Apostolic Foundation of the Christian Church'.

'The Author proceeds to open and allege that Jesus Christ is and ever was *The Son of God*. This greatest of subjects, this most profound of all mysteries, is handled with reverence and with outstanding perception.

'The second part considers *The Seed of David*. What is meant precisely by 'the seed'? And why 'of David'? With prophetic insight the author expounds these essential verities.'

Price £6.95 (*postage extra*)
Hardback 250 pages
Laminated bookjacket
Printed, sewn and bound
by the John Metcalfe Publishing Trust
ISBN 978 1 870039 16 1

CHRIST CRUCIFIED

THE APOSTOLIC FOUNDATION
OF THE
CHRISTIAN CHURCH

Volume V

Christ Crucified, the definitive work on the crucifixion, the blood, and the cross of Jesus Christ.

The crucifixion of Jesus Christ witnessed in the Gospels: the gospel according to Matthew; Mark; Luke; John.

The blood of Jesus Christ declared in the Epistles: the shed blood; the blood of purchase; redemption through his blood; the blood of sprinkling; the blood of the covenant.

The doctrine of the cross revealed in the apostolic foundation of the Christian church: the doctrine of the cross; the cross and the body of sin; the cross and the carnal mind; the cross and the law; the offence of the cross; the cross of our Lord Jesus Christ.

Price £6.95 *(postage extra)*
Hardback 300 pages
Laminated bookjacket
Printed, sewn and bound
by the John Metcalfe Publishing Trust
ISBN 978 1 870039 08 6

JUSTIFICATION BY FAITH

THE APOSTOLIC FOUNDATION
OF THE
CHRISTIAN CHURCH

Volume VI

THE HEART OF THE GOSPEL · THE FOUNDATION OF THE CHURCH
THE ISSUE OF ETERNITY
CLEARLY, ORIGINALLY AND POWERFULLY OPENED

The basis · The righteousness of the law
The righteousness of God · The atonement · Justification
Traditional views considered · Righteousness imputed to faith
Faith counted for righteousness · Justification by Faith

'And it came to pass, when Jesus had ended these sayings, the people were astonished at his doctrine: for he taught them as one having authority, and not as the scribes', Matthew 7:28,29.

Price £7.50 (*postage extra*)
Hardback 375 pages
Laminated bookjacket
Printed, sewn and bound
by the John Metcalfe Publishing Trust
ISBN 978 1 870039 11 6

THE CHURCH: WHAT IS IT?

THE APOSTOLIC FOUNDATION
OF THE
CHRISTIAN CHURCH

Volume VII

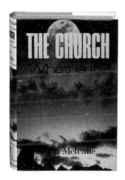

The answer to this question proceeds first from the lips of Jesus himself, Mt. 16:18, later to be expounded by the words of the apostles whom he sent.

Neither fear of man nor favour from the world remotely affect the answer.

Here is the truth, the whole truth, and nothing but the truth.

The complete originality, the vast range, and the total fearlessness of this book command the attention in a way that is unique.

Read this book: you will never read another like it.

Outspokenly devastating yet devastatingly constructive.

Price £7.75 (postage extra)
Hardback 400 pages
Laminated bookjacket
Printed, sewn and bound
by the John Metcalfe Publishing Trust
ISBN 978 1 870039 23 9

THE REVELATION OF JESUS CHRIST

THE APOSTOLIC FOUNDATION
OF THE
CHRISTIAN CHURCH

Volume VIII

Uniquely perceptive and original, the result of decades alone in the secret place of the most High, abiding under the shadow of the Almighty, this peerless work on the Revelation of Jesus Christ will stand the test of time and eternity for its heavenly, spiritual, and divine opening into the last book of the last apostle of the new testament, for all who have an ear to hear what the Spirit saith unto the churches.

Here is the transcript of the series of addresses delivered over some eighteen months during 1997 and 1998, in the Assembly Hall, Church House, Westminster, London, by John Metcalfe.

The famed Assembly Hall is used as the Synod Chamber of the Church of England as occasion requires.

Price £9.25 (*postage extra*)
Hardback 640 pages
Laminated bookjacket
Printed, sewn and bound
by the John Metcalfe Publishing Trust
ISBN 978 1 870039 77 2

THE MINISTRY OF RECONCILIATION

THE APOSTOLIC FOUNDATION
OF THE
CHRISTIAN CHURCH

Volume IX

THE MINISTRY OF RECONCILIATION

The Implication of Reconciliation · The Ministry of Reconciliation
The Tenses in Reconciliation · The Scope of Reconciliation
The Ground of Reconciliation

THE MEANING OF 'RECONCILIATION'

THE NATURE OF RECONCILIATION

The Substitution · The Doctrine
The Premise: Adam and Christ, Romans 5:12-14
The Three Comparisons, Romans 5:15-17
The Two Deductions, Romans 5:18-19
Parenthesis: The Law, verse 20 · The Conclusion, Romans 5:21

Price £6.95 (*postage extra*)
Hardback 270 pages
Laminated bookjacket
Printed, sewn and bound
by the John Metcalfe Publishing Trust
ISBN 978 1 870039 87 1

SALVATION

THE APOSTOLIC FOUNDATION
OF THE
CHRISTIAN CHURCH

Volume X

SALVATION FROM SIN
Wilful Sins · The Remission of Sins · Inbred Sin

SALVATION FROM SATAN
The 'Satan' · The 'Devil' · The 'Prince' · The 'Serpent'

SALVATION FROM THE WORLD
Salvation from the World:
'Aiōn' · 'Gē' · 'Oikoumenē' · 'Kosmos'

SALVATION FROM THE WRATH TO COME
'Thumos' and 'Orgē' · 'Sheol'; 'Hadēs'; 'Gehenna'
The Meaning of the Words
Figures of the True · Salvation from Wrath

Price £9.25 (postage extra)
Hardback 500 pages
Laminated bookjacket
Printed, sewn and bound
by the John Metcalfe Publishing Trust
ISBN 978 1 870039 88 8

LECTURES
FROM
CHURCH HOUSE, WESTMINSTER

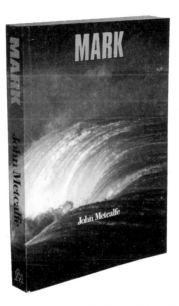

PHILEMON

This penetrating revelation of the Epistle to Philemon opens the substance of four consecutive lectures given by John Metcalfe in The Hoare Memorial Hall, Church House, Westminster, London.

Price £1.90 (*postage extra*)
Paperback 190 pages (Laminated cover)
Printed, sewn and bound
by the John Metcalfe Publishing Trust
ISBN 978 1 870039 66 6

FIRST TIMOTHY

This penetrating revelation of the First Epistle to Timothy opens the substance of five consecutive lectures given by John Metcalfe in The Hoare Memorial Hall, Church House, Westminster, London.

Price £2.00 (*postage extra*)
Paperback 220 pages (Laminated cover)
Printed, sewn and bound
by the John Metcalfe Publishing Trust
ISBN 978 1 870039 67 3

NEWLY REPUBLISHED
Second Edition
Over five thousand copies sold

THE EVANGEL
ACCORDING TO MATTHEW

This concise revelation of the essence and structure of the
Evangel according to Matthew, the culmination of years of
prayer and devotion, retreat and study, opens the mind of the
Spirit in the unique vision of Jesus Christ, the son of David,
the son of Abraham, recorded in the first gospel.

Price £1.45p *(postage extra)*
Paperback 135 pages (Laminated cover)
Printed, sewn and bound
by the John Metcalfe Publishing Trust
ISBN 978 1 870039 73 4

Fifth Printing
Over twenty thousand copies sold

CREATION

Genesis 1:1, 'In the beginning God created the heaven and the earth.'

This spiritually penetrating and outstandingly original revelation of the Creation from Genesis chapters 1 and 2 opens the substance of five consecutive lectures given by John Metcalfe, commencing in the Hoare Memorial Hall and later moving to the central Assembly Hall, Church House, Westminster, London.

The Hoare Memorial Hall was used as the House of Commons at various times during the Second World War. Many of Sir Winston Churchill's renowned war time speeches were delivered in this Hall. The famed Assembly Hall is used as the Synod Chamber of the Church of England as occasion requires.

Price £2.00 *(postage extra)*
Paperback 230 pages (Laminated cover)
Printed, sewn and bound
by the John Metcalfe Publishing Trust
ISBN 978 1 870039 71 0

NEWLY REPUBLISHED
Second Printing
Over five thousand copies sold

COLOSSIANS

This concise and unique revelation of the Epistle to the
Colossians has the hallmark of spiritual originality and insight
peculiar to the ministry of John Metcalfe. It is as if a diamond,
inert and lifeless in itself, has been divinely cut at great cost,
so that every way in which it is turned, the light from above is
enhanced and magnified to break forth with divine radiance
showing colour and depth hitherto unsuspected.

Price 95p *(postage extra)*
Paperback 135 pages (Laminated cover)
Printed, sewn and bound
by the John Metcalfe Publishing Trust
ISBN 978 1 870039 55 0

PHILIPPIANS

The Epistle of Paul the Apostle to the Philippians is opened by this work from the pen of John Metcalfe with that lucid thoroughness which one has come to expect from a ministry received 'not of men, neither by man, but by the revelation of Jesus Christ'.

The work of God at Philippi is traced 'from the first day' until the time at which the epistle was written. Never was Lydia or the Philippian jailor drawn with more lively insight. The epistle itself is revealed in order, with passages–such as 'the mind that was in Christ Jesus'–that evidence the work of no less than a divine for our own times.

Price £1.90 *(postage extra)*
Paperback 185 pages (Laminated cover)
Printed, sewn and bound
by the John Metcalfe Publishing Trust
ISBN 978 1 870039 56 7

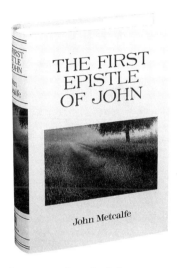

XXX

OTHER TITLES

Second Edition
Sixth Printing
Over twenty thousand copies sold

NOAH AND THE FLOOD

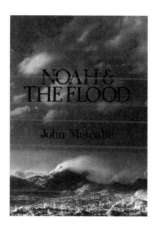

Noah and the Flood expounds with vital urgency the man and the message that heralded the end of the old world. The description of the flood itself is vividly realistic. The whole work has an unmistakable ring of authority, and speaks as 'Thus saith the Lord'.

'Mr. Metcalfe makes a skilful use of persuasive eloquence as he challenges the reality of one's profession of faith ... he gives a rousing call to a searching self-examination and evaluation of one's spiritual experience.'

The Monthly Record of the Free Church of Scotland.

Price £2.40 (*postage extra*)
Paperback 155 pages (Laminated cover)
Printed, sewn and bound
by the John Metcalfe Publishing Trust
ISBN 978 1 870039 22 2

Second Edition
Over five thousand copies sold

DIVINE FOOTSTEPS

Divine Footsteps traces the pathway of the feet of the Son of man from the very beginning in the prophetic figures of the true in the old testament through the reality in the new; doing so in a way of experimental spirituality. At the last a glimpse of the coming glory is beheld as his feet are viewed as standing at the latter day upon the earth.

Price 95p *(postage extra)*
Paperback 120 pages (Laminated cover)
Printed, sewn and bound
by the John Metcalfe Publishing Trust
ISBN 978 1 870039 21 5

OF GOD OR MAN?

LIGHT FROM GALATIANS

The Epistle to the Galatians contends for deliverance from the law and from carnal ministry.

The Apostle opens his matter in two ways:

Firstly, Paul vindicates himself and his ministry against those that came not from God above, but from Jerusalem below.

Secondly, he defends the Gospel and evangelical liberty against legal perversions and bondage to the flesh.

Price £1.45 *(postage extra)*
Paperback 190 pages (Laminated cover)
ISBN 978 0 9506366 3 4

Second Edition
Third Printing

Over ten thousand copies sold

THE RED HEIFER

The Red Heifer was the name given to a sacrifice used by the children of Israel in the Old Testament – as recorded in Numbers 19 – in which a heifer was slain and burned. Cedar wood, hyssop and scarlet were cast into the burning, and the ashes were mingled with running water and put in a vessel. It was kept for the children of Israel for a water of separation: it was a purification for sin.

In this unusual book the sacrifice is brought up to date and its relevance to the church today is shown.

Price 95p *(postage extra)*
Paperback 120 pages (Laminated cover)
Printed, sewn and bound
by the John Metcalfe Publishing Trust
ISBN 978 1 870039 89 5

A QUESTION FOR POPE JOHN PAUL II

As a consequence of his many years spent apart in prayer, lonely vigil, and painstaking study of the scripture, John Metcalfe asked a question but looked in vain for an answer from Pope John Paul II. Now the question hangs still unanswered before a higher and ultimate Authority.

Price £1.25 *(postage extra)*
Paperback 105 pages (Laminated cover)
ISBN 978 0 9506366 4 1

THE BOOK OF RUTH

The Book of Ruth is set against the farming background of old testament Israel at the time of the Judges, the narrative—unfolding the work of God in redemption—being marked by a series of agricultural events.

These events—the famine; the barley harvest; the wheat harvest; the winnowing—possessed a hidden spiritual significance to that community, but, much more, they speak in figure directly to our own times, as the book reveals.

Equally contemporary appear the characters of Ruth, Naomi, Boaz, and the first kinsman, drawn with spiritual perception greatly to the profit of the reader.

Price £4.95 (*postage extra*)
Hardback 200 pages
Laminated bookjacket
Printed, sewn and bound
by the John Metcalfe Publishing Trust
ISBN 978 1 870039 17 8

DIVINE MEDITATIONS

OF

WILLIAM HUNTINGTON

Originally published by Mr. Huntington as a series of letters to J. Jenkins, under the title of 'Contemplations on the God of Israel', the spiritual content of this correspondence has been skilfully and sympathetically edited, abridged, and arranged so as to form a series of meditations, suitable for daily readings.

Mr. Huntington's own text is thereby adapted to speak directly to the reader in a way much more suited to his ministering immediately to ourselves, in our own circumstances and times.

It is greatly hoped that many today will benefit from this adaptation which carefully retains both the spirit and the letter of the text. If any prefer the original format, this is readily available from several sources and many libraries.

Nevertheless, the publishers believe the much more readable form into which Mr. Huntington's very words have been adapted will appeal to a far wider audience, for whose comfort and consolation this carefully edited work has been published.

Price £2.35 (*postage extra*)
Paperback 300 pages (Laminated cover)
Printed, sewn and bound
by the John Metcalfe Publishing Trust
ISBN 978 1 870039 24 6

SAVING FAITH

The sevenfold work of the Holy Ghost in bringing a sinner to saving faith in Christ opened and enlarged.

True faith is the work of God. False faith is the presumption of man. But where is the difference? *Saving Faith* shows the difference.

Price £2.25 (*postage extra*)
Paperback 250 pages (Laminated cover)
Printed, sewn and bound
by the John Metcalfe Publishing Trust
ISBN 978 1 870039 40 6

PRESENT-DAY CONVERSIONS
OF THE NEW TESTAMENT KIND

FROM THE MINISTRY OF

JOHN METCALFE

The outstandingly striking presentation of this fascinating paperback will surely catch the eye, as its title and contents will certainly captivate the mind: here is a unique publication.

Woven into a gripping narrative, over twenty-one short life stories, all centred on conversions that simply could not have happened had not God broken in, and had not Christ been revealed, the book presents a tremendous challenge, at once moving and thrilling to the reader.

Price £2.25 (*postage extra*)
Paperback 240 pages (Laminated cover)
Printed, sewn and bound
by the John Metcalfe Publishing Trust
ISBN 978 1 870039 31 4

Second Edition
Third Printing
Over ten thousand copies sold

THE WELLS OF SALVATION

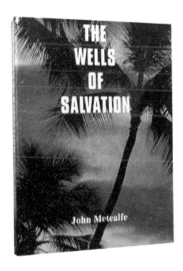

The Wells of Salvation is written from a series of seven powerful addresses preached at Tylers Green. It is a forthright and experimental exposition of Isaiah 12:3, 'Therefore with joy shall ye draw water out of the wells of salvation.'

John Metcalfe is acknowledged to be perhaps the most gifted expositor and powerful preacher of our day and this is to be seen clearly in The Wells of Salvation.

Price £2.35 *(postage extra)*
Paperback 285 pages (Laminated cover)
Printed, sewn and bound
by the John Metcalfe Publishing Trust
ISBN 978 1 870039 72 7

PASTORAL LETTERS TO THE FAR EAST

Feeling the abiding spiritual value of letters written by John Metcalfe in his absence from the Far East, Miss Sie Siok Hui cherished the correspondence to her, and at the same time was moved to seek for similar writings to some of her closest sisters in Christ.

Gathering these letters together, it was her earnest desire that such an enduring testimony should be made available to all the faithful remnant in our own day. The result of her prayers and spiritual exercise appears in the publication 'Pastoral Letters to the Far East'.

Price £2.00 *(postage extra)*
Paperback 240 pages (Laminated cover)
Printed, sewn and bound
by the John Metcalfe Publishing Trust
ISBN 978 1 870039 74 1

DELIVERANCE FROM THE LAW
THE WESTMINSTER CONFESSION EXPLODED

Deliverance from the Law. A devastating vindication of the gospel of Christ against the traditions of man.

Price £1.90 *(postage extra)*
Paperback 160 pages (Laminated cover)
Printed, sewn and bound
by the John Metcalfe Publishing Trust
ISBN 978 1 870039 41 3

NEWLY REPUBLISHED
Second Printing
Over five thousand copies sold

THE BEATITUDES

A unique insight destined to be the classic opening of this wonderful sequence of utterances from the lips of Jesus.

The reader will discover a penetration of the spiritual heights and divine depths of these peerless words in a way ever fresh and always rewarding though read time and time again.

Price £2.40 *(postage extra)*
Paperback 185 pages (Laminated cover)
Printed, sewn and bound
by the John Metcalfe Publishing Trust
ISBN 978 1 870039 45 1

xli

LAW AND GRACE CONTRASTED

A SERIES OF ADDRESSES

BY

WILLIAM HUNTINGTON

The Child of Liberty in Legal Bondage · The Bondchild
brought to the Test · The Modern Plasterer Detected
Not under Law · The Law a Rule of Life?

Mr. Huntington's own text is adapted to speak directly to the
reader in a way much more suited to his ministering immediately to ourselves, in our own circumstances and times.

It is greatly hoped that many today will benefit from this
adaptation which carefully retains both the spirit and the letter
of the text. If any prefer the original format, this is readily
available from several sources and many libraries.

Nevertheless, the publishers believe the much more readable
form into which Mr. Huntington's very words have been
adapted will appeal to a far wider audience, for whose comfort
and consolation this carefully edited work has been published.

Price £2.35 (*postage extra*)
Paperback 265 pages (Laminated cover)
Printed, sewn and bound
by the John Metcalfe Publishing Trust
ISBN 978 1 870039 76 5

NEWLY REPUBLISHED
Second Printing
Over five thousand copies sold

THE GIFTS AND BAPTISM
OF THE SPIRIT

John Metcalfe

Companion Volume to 'The Body of Christ and the Gifts'

For so long confusion has reigned in respect of THE GIFTS AND
BAPTISM OF THE SPIRIT. Here at last is that spiritual, sound, and
balanced opening of the Holy Scripture from I Corinthians 12:1-13.

This gives the unmistakable ring of apostolic authority, puts the
matter beyond the realm of speculation or experiment, past all
doubt bringing the text into the light of revelation of Jesus Christ.

Price £1.45 (*postage extra*)
Paperback 128 pages (Laminated cover)
Printed, sewn and bound
by the John Metcalfe Publishing Trust
ISBN 978 1 870039 80 2

THE COMING RESURRECTION OF THE DEAD

John Metcalfe

For so long confusion has reigned in respect of THE COMING RESURRECTION OF THE DEAD. Here at last is that spiritual, sound, and balanced opening of the Holy Scripture from I Corinthians 15.

This gives the unmistakable ring of apostolic authority, puts the matter beyond the realm of speculation or prejudice, past all doubt bringing the text into the light of revelation of Jesus Christ.

Price 95p (*postage extra*)
Paperback 145 pages (Laminated cover)
Printed, sewn and bound
by the John Metcalfe Publishing Trust
ISBN 978 1 870039 85 7

THE BODY OF CHRIST
AND THE GIFTS

For so long confusion has reigned in respect of THE BODY OF CHRIST AND THE GIFTS. Here at last is that spiritual, sound, and balanced opening of the Holy Scripture from I Corinthians 12:14-13:13.

This gives the unmistakable ring of apostolic authority, puts the matter beyond the realm of speculation or experiment, past all doubt bringing the text into the light of revelation of Jesus Christ.

Price 95p (*postage extra*)
Paperback 140 pages (Laminated cover)
Printed, sewn and bound
by the John Metcalfe Publishing Trust
ISBN 978 1 870039 82 6

Second printing
Over five thousand copies sold

THE GIFTS OF TONGUES
AND OF PROPHECY

For so long confusion has reigned in respect of THE GIFTS OF TONGUES AND OF PROPHECY. Here at last is that spiritual, sound, and balanced opening of the Holy Scripture from I Corinthians 14.

This gives the unmistakable ring of apostolic authority, puts the matter beyond the realm of speculation or experiment, past all doubt bringing the text into the light of revelation of Jesus Christ.

Price 95p (*postage extra*)
Paperback 90 pages (Laminated cover)
Printed, sewn and bound
by the John Metcalfe Publishing Trust
ISBN 978 1 870039 86 4

OPENINGS IN
FIRST CORINTHIANS

THE BEGINNING · THE VISION
THE OPENING: THE TESTIMONY OF CHRIST

JUDGMENT CONCERNING THE TESTIMONY:

Judgment concerning divisions; Judgment concerning the wicked; Judgment pertaining to the saints; Judgment concerning questions of marriage; Judgment concerning meats offered to idols; Judgment concerning headship.

JUDGMENT CONCERNING ASSEMBLING TOGETHER:

The Lord's Supper; The Unity of the Spirit in the Body of Christ; The manifestation of the Gifts in the Assembly; The Evangelical Truth of the Resurrection of the Dead.

THE CONCLUSION

Price £9.25 (*postage extra*)
Hardback 495 pages
Laminated bookjacket
Printed, sewn and bound
by the John Metcalfe Publishing Trust

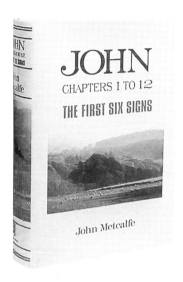

'TRACT FOR THE TIMES' SERIES

The Gospel of God by John Metcalfe. No. 1 in the Series. Laminated cover, price 25p.

The Strait Gate by John Metcalfe. No. 2 in the Series. Laminated cover, price 25p.

Eternal Sonship and Taylor Brethren by John Metcalfe. No. 3 in the Series. Laminated cover, price 25p.

Marks of the New Testament Church by John Metcalfe. No. 4 in the Series. Laminated cover, price 25p.

The Charismatic Delusion by John Metcalfe. No. 5 in the Series. Laminated cover, price 25p.

Premillennialism Exposed by John Metcalfe. No. 6 in the Series. Laminated cover, price 25p.

Justification and Peace by John Metcalfe. No. 7 in the Series. Laminated cover, price 25p.

Faith or Presumption? by John Metcalfe. No. 8 in the Series. Laminated cover, price 25p.

The Elect Undeceived by John Metcalfe. No. 9 in the Series. Laminated cover, price 25p.

Justifying Righteousness by John Metcalfe. No. 10 in the Series. Laminated cover, price 25p.

Righteousness Imputed by John Metcalfe. No. 11 in the Series. Laminated cover, price 25p.

The Great Deception by John Metcalfe. No. 12 in the Series. Laminated cover, price 25p.

A Famine in the Land by John Metcalfe. No. 13 in the Series. Laminated cover, price 25p.

Blood and Water by John Metcalfe. No. 14 in the Series. Laminated cover, price 25p.

Women Bishops? by John Metcalfe. No. 15 in the Series. Laminated cover, price 25p.

The Heavenly Vision by John Metcalfe. No. 16 in the Series. Laminated cover, price 25p.

The Mystery of Godliness by John Metcalfe. No. 17 in the Series. Laminated cover, price 25p.

EVANGELICAL TRACTS

1. **The Two Prayers of Elijah.** Light green card cover, price 10p.

2. **Wounded for our Transgressions.** Gold card cover, price 10p.

3. **The Blood of Sprinkling.** Red card cover, price 10p.

4. **The Grace of God that brings Salvation.** Blue card cover, price 10p.

5. **The Name of Jesus.** Rose card cover, price 10p.

6. **The Ministry of the New Testament.** Purple card cover, price 10p.

7. **The Death of the Righteous** (*The closing days of J.B. Stoney*) by A.M.S. (his daughter). Ivory card cover, price 10p.

8. **Repentance.** Sky blue card cover, price 10p.

9. **Legal Deceivers Exposed**. Crimson card cover, price 10p.

10. **Unconditional Salvation.** Green card cover, price 10p.

11. **Religious Merchandise.** Brown card cover, price 10p.

12. **Comfort.** Pink card cover, price 10p.

13. **Peace.** Grey card cover, price 10p.

14. **Eternal Life.** Cobalt card cover, price 10p.

15. **The Handwriting of Ordinances.** Fawn card cover, price 10p.

16. **'Lord, Lord!'.** Emerald card cover, price 10p.

17. **Conversion.** Wedgewood card cover, price 10p.

18. **The Calling of John Metcalfe.** Navy blue card cover, price 10p.

ECCLESIA TRACTS

The Beginning of the Ecclesia by John Metcalfe. No. 1 in the Series, Sand grain cover, price 10p.

Churches and the Church by J.N. Darby. Edited. No. 2 in the Series, Sand grain cover, price 10p.

The Ministers of Christ by John Metcalfe. No. 3 in the Series, Sand grain cover, price 10p.

The Inward Witness by George Fox. Edited. No. 4 in the Series, Sand grain cover, price 10p.

The Notion of a Clergyman by J.N. Darby. Edited. No. 5 in the Series, Sand grain cover, price 10p.

The Servant of the Lord by William Huntington. Edited and Abridged. No. 6 in the Series, Sand grain cover, price 10p.

One Spirit by William Kelly. Edited. No. 7 in the Series, Sand grain cover, price 10p.

The Funeral of Arminianism by William Huntington. Edited and Abridged. No. 8 in the Series, Sand grain cover, price 10p.

One Body by William Kelly. Edited. No. 9 in the Series, Sand grain cover, price 10p.

False Churches and True by John Metcalfe. No. 10 in the Series, Sand grain cover, price 10p.

Separation from Evil by J.N. Darby. Edited. No. 11 in the Series, Sand grain cover, price 10p.

The Remnant by J.B. Stoney. Edited. No. 12 in the Series, Sand grain cover, price 10p.

The Arminian Skeleton by William Huntington. Edited and Abridged. No. 13 in the Series, Sand grain cover, price 10p.

FOUNDATION TRACTS

1. **Female Priests?** by John Metcalfe. Oatmeal cover, price 25p.

2. **The Bondage of the Will** by Martin Luther. Translated and Abridged. Oatmeal cover, price 25p.

3. **Of the Popish Mass** by John Calvin. Translated and Abridged. Oatmeal cover, price 25p.

4. **The Adversary** by John Metcalfe. Oatmeal cover, price 25p.

5. **The Advance of Popery** by J.C. Philpot. Oatmeal cover, price 25p.

6. **Enemies in the Land** by John Metcalfe. Oatmeal cover, price 25p.

7. **An Admonition Concerning Relics** by John Calvin. Oatmeal cover, price 25p.

8. **John Metcalfe's Testimony Against Falsity in Worship** by John Metcalfe. Oatmeal cover, price 25p.

9. **Brethrenism Exposed** by John Metcalfe. Oatmeal cover, price 25p.

10. **John Metcalfe's Testimony Against The Social Gospel** by John Metcalfe. Oatmeal cover, price 25p.

MINISTRY BY JOHN METCALFE

TAPE MINISTRY BY JOHN METCALFE
FROM THE U.K. AND THE FAR EAST
IS AVAILABLE

In order to obtain this free recorded ministry, please send your blank cassette (C.90) and the cost of the return postage, including your name and address in block capitals, to the John Metcalfe Publishing Trust, Church Road, Tylers Green, Penn, Bucks, HP10 8LN. Tapelists are available on request.

Owing to the increased demand for the tape ministry, we are unable to supply more than two tapes per order, except in the case of meetings for the hearing of tapes, where a special arrangement can be made.

THE MINISTRY OF THE NEW TESTAMENT

The purpose of this substantial A4 gloss paper magazine is to provide spiritual and experimental ministry with sound doctrine which rightly and prophetically divides the word of truth.

Readers of our books will already know the high standards of our publications. They can be confident that these pages will maintain that quality, by giving access to enduring ministry from the past, much of which is derived from sources that are virtually unobtainable today, and publishing a living ministry from the present. Selected articles from the following writers have already been included:

ELI ASHDOWN · JOHN BERRIDGE · HENRY BIRCH · ABRAHAM BOOTH
JAMES BOURNE · JOHN BRADFORD · WILLIAM BRIDGE
JOHN BUNYAN · JOHN BURGON · WILLIAM CHALMERS BURNS
JOHN CALVIN · DONALD CARGILL · JOHN CENNICK · J.N. DARBY
EBENEZER ERSKINE · RALPH ERSKINE · GEORGE FOX · JOHN FOXE
WILLIAM GADSBY · JOHN GIBBS · BERNARD GILPIN · JOHN GUTHRIE
WILLIAM GUTHRIE · GREY HAZLERIGG · JOHN HICKS
WILLIAM HUNTINGTON · WILLIAM KELLY · JOHN KENNEDY
JOHN KERSHAW · JOHN KEYT · HANSERD KNOLLYS · JOHN KNOX
JAMES LEWIS · MARTIN LUTHER · ROBERT MURRAY MCCHEYNE
JOHN METCALFE · BROWNLOW NORTH · THOMAS OXENHAM
ALEXANDER–SANDY–PEDEN · J.C. PHILPOT · J.K. POPHAM
JAMES RENWICK · SAMUEL RUTHERFORD · J.B. STONEY
HENRY TANNER · WILLIAM TIPTAFT · ARTHUR TRIGGS
JOHN VINALL · JOHN WARBURTON · JOHN WELWOOD · JAMES WEST
GEORGE WHITEFIELD · THOMAS WILCOX · J.A. WYLIE

Price £1.75 (postage included)
Issued Spring, Summer, Autumn, Winter.

Magazine Order Form

Name and address (in block capitals)

....

....

....

Please send me ...... current copy/copies of The Ministry of the New Testament.

Please send me ...... year/s subscription.

I enclose a cheque/postal order for £......

(Price: including postage, U.K. £1.75; Overseas £1.90)
(One year's subscription: including postage, U.K. £7.00; Overseas £7.60)

Cheques should be made payable to The John Metcalfe Publishing Trust, and for overseas subscribers should be in pounds sterling drawn on a London Bank.

10 or more copies to one address will qualify for a 10% discount.

Some back numbers from Spring 1986 available.

Please send to The John Metcalfe Publishing Trust, Church Road, Tylers Green, Penn, Bucks, HP10 8LN, U.K.

All publications of the Trust are subsidised by the Publishers

Book Order Form

Please send to the address below:

	Price	Quantity
A Question for Pope John Paul II	£1.25	......
Of God or Man?	£1.45	......
Noah and the Flood	£1.90	......
Divine Footsteps	£0.95	......
The Red Heifer	£0.95	......
The Wells of Salvation	£2.35	......
The Book of Ruth (Hardback edition)	£4.95	......
Divine Meditations of William Huntington	£2.35	......
Present-Day Conversions of the New Testament Kind	£2.25	......
Saving Faith	£2.25	......
Deliverance from the Law	£1.90	......
The Beatitudes	£2.40	......
Pastoral Letters to the Far East	£2.00	......
Law and Grace Contrasted by William Huntington	£2.35	......
The Gifts and Baptism of the Spirit	£1.45	......
The Body of Christ and the Gifts	£0.95	......
The Coming Resurrection of the Dead	£0.95	......
The Gifts of Tongues and of Prophecy	£0.95	......
Openings in First Corinthians (Hardback edition)	£9.25	......
John Chapters 1-12 The First Six Signs (Hardback edition)	£9.25	......

Lectures from Church House, Westminster

	Price	Quantity
Colossians	£0.95	......
Philippians	£1.90	......
Matthew	£1.45	......
Philemon	£1.90	......
First Timothy	£2.00	......
Mark	£2.35	......
Creation	£2.00	......
The First Epistle of John (Hardback edition)	£9.25	......

Psalms, Hymns & Spiritual Songs (Hardback edition)

	Price	Quantity
The Psalms of the Old Testament	£4.25	......
Spiritual Songs from the Four Evangelists	£2.50	......
The Hymns of the New Testament	£2.50	......

'Apostolic Foundation of the Christian Church' series

		Price	Quantity
Foundations Uncovered	Vol. I	£0.75	......
The Birth of Jesus Christ	Vol. II	£0.95	......
The Messiah (Hardback edition)	Vol. III	£7.75	......
The Son of God and Seed of David (Hardback edition)	Vol. IV	£6.95	......
Christ Crucified (Hardback edition)	Vol. V	£6.95	......
Justification by Faith (Hardback edition)	Vol. VI	£7.50	......
The Church: What is it? (Hardback edition)	Vol. VII	£7.75	......
The Revelation of Jesus Christ (Hardback edition)	Vol. VIII	£9.25	......
The Ministry of Reconciliation (Hardback edition)	Vol. IX	£6.95	......
Salvation (Hardback edition)	Vol. X	£9.25	......

Name and address (in block capitals)

....

....

....

If money is sent with order please allow for postage. Please address to:- The
John Metcalfe Publishing Trust, Church Road, Tylers Green, Penn, Bucks, HP10 8LN, U.K.

cut here

Tract Order Form

Please send to the address below:

Price   Quantity

Evangelical Tracts

	Price	Quantity
The Two Prayers of Elijah	£0.10	......
Wounded for our Transgressions	£0.10	......
The Blood of Sprinkling	£0.10	......
The Grace of God that brings Salvation	£0.10	......
The Name of Jesus	£0.10	......
The Ministry of the New Testament	£0.10	......
The Death of the Righteous by A.M.S.	£0.10	......
Repentance	£0.10	......
Legal Deceivers Exposed	£0.10	......
Unconditional Salvation	£0.10	......
Religious Merchandise	£0.10	......
Comfort	£0.10	......
Peace	£0.10	......
Eternal Life	£0.10	......
The Handwriting of Ordinances	£0.10	......
'Lord, Lord!'	£0.10	......
Conversion	£0.10	......
The Calling of John Metcalfe	£0.10	......

'Tract for the Times' series

		Price	Quantity
The Gospel of God	No. 1	£0.25	......
The Strait Gate	No. 2	£0.25	......
Eternal Sonship and Taylor Brethren	No. 3	£0.25	......
Marks of the New Testament Church	No. 4	£0.25	......
The Charismatic Delusion	No. 5	£0.25	......
Premillennialism Exposed	No. 6	£0.25	......
Justification and Peace	No. 7	£0.25	......
Faith or Presumption?	No. 8	£0.25	......
The Elect Undeceived	No. 9	£0.25	......
Justifying Righteousness	No.10	£0.25	......
Righteousness Imputed	No.11	£0.25	......
The Great Deception	No.12	£0.25	......
A Famine in the Land	No.13	£0.25	......
Blood and Water	No.14	£0.25	......
Women Bishops?	No.15	£0.25	......
The Heavenly Vision	No.16	£0.25	......
The Mystery of Godliness	No.17	£0.25	......

Name and address (in block capitals)

....

....

....

If money is sent with order please allow for postage. Please address to:- The John Metcalfe Publishing Trust, Church Road, Tylers Green, Penn, Bucks, HP10 8LN, U.K.

cut here

Tract Order Form

Please send to the address below:

		Price	Quantity
Ecclesia Tracts			
The Beginning of the Ecclesia	No. 1	£0.10	......
Churches and the Church (J.N.D.)	No. 2	£0.10	......
The Ministers of Christ	No. 3	£0.10	......
The Inward Witness (G.F.)	No. 4	£0.10	......
The Notion of a Clergyman (J.N.D.)	No. 5	£0.10	......
The Servant of the Lord (W.H.)	No. 6	£0.10	......
One Spirit (W.K.)	No. 7	£0.10	......
The Funeral of Arminianism (W.H.)	No. 8	£0.10	......
One Body (W.K.)	No. 9	£0.10	......
False Churches and True	No.10	£0.10	......
Separation from Evil (J.N.D.)	No.11	£0.10	......
The Remnant (J.B.S.)	No.12	£0.10	......
The Arminian Skeleton (W.H.)	No.13	£0.10	......
Foundation Tracts			
Female Priests?	No. 1	£0.25	......
The Bondage of the Will (Martin Luther)	No. 2	£0.25	......
Of the Popish Mass (John Calvin)	No. 3	£0.25	......
The Adversary	No. 4	£0.25	......
The Advance of Popery (J.C. Philpot)	No. 5	£0.25	......
Enemies in the Land	No. 6	£0.25	......
An Admonition Concerning Relics (John Calvin)	No. 7	£0.25	......
John Metcalfe's Testimony Against Falsity in Worship	No. 8	£0.25	......
Brethrenism Exposed	No. 9	£0.25	......
John Metcalfe's Testimony Against The Social Gospel	No.10	£0.25	......

Name and address (in block capitals)

....

....

....

If money is sent with order please allow for postage. Please address to:- The
John Metcalfe Publishing Trust, Church Road, Tylers Green, Penn, Bucks, HP10 8LN, U.K.

cut here

lxvi